Money Around the World

Saving Money

Rebecca Rissman

Heinemann
LIBRARY

www.heinemann.co.uk/library

Visit our website to find out more information about Heinemann Library books.

To order:

☎ Phone 44 (0) 1865 888066

▤ Send a fax to 44 (0) 1865 314091

▢ Visit the Heinemann Bookshop at www.heinemann.co.uk/library to browse our catalogue and order online.

First published in Great Britain by Heinemann Library, Halley Court, Jordan Hill, Oxford OX2 8EJ, part of Harcourt Education. Heinemann is a registered trademark of Harcourt Education Ltd.

Editorial: Diyan Leake
Design: Joanna Hinton-Malivoire and Steve Mead
Picture Research: Tracy Cummins and Heather Mauldin
Production: Duncan Gilbert

Origination: Chroma Graphics (Overseas) Pte Ltd
Printed and bound in China by South China Printing Company Ltd

ISBN 978 0 431 02525 4
12 11 10 09 08
10 9 8 7 6 5 4 3 2 1

British Library Cataloguing in Publication Data

Rissman, Rebecca
Saving money. - (Money around the world)
1. Saving and investment - Juvenile literature
I. Title
332'.0415

Acknowledgments

The author and publisher are grateful to the following for permission to reproduce copyright material: © Age Fotostock pp. **10**, **17** (Picture Partners), **20** (Glowimages), **23a** (Flying Colours Ltd), **back cover** (Flying Colours Ltd); © Alamy pp. **5** (Peter Titmuss), **18** (Rob Walls), **19** (Peerpoint); © Corbis p. **6** (Ronnie Kaufman); © Getty Images pp. **4** (Nick Dolding), **7** (AFP/Teh Eng Koon), **8** (Kristjan Maack), **11** (Robert Nickelsberg), **12**, **13** (AFP/Saif Dahlah **14** (Yann Layma), **15** (Ken Chernus), **16**, **21** (Elyse Lewin), **22a** (Nick Dolding), **23b** (Don Smetzer), **23c** (Zubin Shroff); © The World Bank pp. **9**, **22b** (Eric Miller).

Cover photograph reproduced with permission of © agefotostock (Angelika Antl).

Every effort has been made to contact copyright holders of any material reproduced in this book. Any omissions will be rectified in subsequent printings if notice is given to the publisher.

Contents

Saving money

People can save money.

People save money to buy
things later.

People save money to buy big things.

People save money to buy
little things.

People save money for a short time.

People save money for a long time.

People save money in jars.

People save money in banks.

Buying things you need

People save money to buy things they need.

People need food.

People need clothes.

People need a place to live.

Buying things you want

People save money to buy things they want.

People save money to buy toys.

People save money to buy books.

People save money to go on holiday.

Money around the world

All around the world, people save money.

What would you save money for?

Places people can save money

◀ Money Jar

◀ Bank

Picture glossary

 **needs** what people must have. Food, clothing, and housing are needs.

 **save** keep for later

 **wants** what people do not need. We do not need toys, holidays, or TVs but we do want them.

Index

Notes for parents and teachers

Before reading

Ask the children if they know what a bank is. Do they have a money box? Talk about why people put money in a bank or money box.

After reading

• Make a chart with the headings: "Needs" and "Wants". Tell the children to look through catalogues and magazines and to cut out pictures of items. Discuss which heading the items should go under.

• Make a money box. Use a tin with a plastic lid (make sure there are no sharp edges). Cut a slot in the lid for each child's money box. Cut a length of paper to wrap around the tin. Tell the children to decorate the paper with pictures of money and glue the paper round the tin.

• Say the nursery rhyme: "Sing a Song of Sixpence".